Douglas Campbell

Central New York in the Revolution

Douglas Campbell

Central New York in the Revolution

ISBN/EAN: 9783337337032

Printed in Europe, USA, Canada, Australia, Japan

Cover: Foto ©ninafisch / pixelio.de

More available books at **www.hansebooks.com**

IN THE

REVOLUTION.

An Address delivered August 15th, 1878, at the unveiling of a
Monument in commemoration of the Massacre
at Cherry Valley, New York in 1778.

By DOUGLAS CAMPBELL.

NEW YORK:

F. J. FICKER, LAW & JOB PRINTER,
Nos. 79 & 81 William St.

1878.

I am very glad that we have met to-day to unveil a monument, and not to lay its corner-stone. The country is dotted all over with the corner-stones of pretentious structures, which, judging from the history of the past, will never be completed. You, with what I think is greater wisdom, have built your modest monument and deferred all ceremonies until its actual completion.

Thirty-eight years ago this little valley was filled with a multitude gathered from all quarters of the union to celebrate the centennial of the settlement of Cherry Valley. William H. Seward, then the Governor of the State, and who since has died full of years and honors, graced the scene with his presence and added to its interest by one of his eloquent speeches. There was also present the Rev. Doctor Nott, who began his career as a minister in this hamlet, and who afterwards, as President of Union College, placed the stamp of his character upon the minds of more than two generations of the leading men of the United States. The chief address upon that occasion was delivered by a native-born son of Cherry Valley, who years before had gathered up the scattered documents and vanishing traditions relating to its history, and woven them into a permanent record. Speaking of the event which we commemorate, he expressed regret that this place was not marked by a fitting monument. To-day he has his wish. The intervening years have brought to him many joys and honors, but I question whether they have borne a more gratifying moment than the present.

We have come together, not to celebrate a victory, but to commemorate a tragedy—a tragedy which blotted from existence the settlement in this valley, and gave back its fields and forests to the wolf and red man. If this were all of the story, we might feel a pang of sorrow, even after a hundred years, as we thought of the desolation of those early settlers,

but history would scarcely have noticed the event. All over the land, from Maine to California, houses have been burned, farms have been ravaged, and hamlets have been blotted out by the destroying savage. From the first advent of the white man to these shores, such tragedies have formed the sad refrain of our frontier annals. The greed of the European, his disregard of justice, and even of plighted faith, his wild rioting in unbridled power, have brought upon him at times the vengeance of a race whose warriors boast as trophies the scalps of women and helpless babes. Trace back the colonial history of the country, and we find the same record which the West presents to-day, where the plundered, half-starved wards of the nation, when they can bear no more, break out in the frenzy of despair.

The Puritans of New England applied to the red man all the prophecies and imprecations which the Old Testament launched against the heathen. They stripped them of their lands, as remorselessly as the chosen people spoiled the Egyptians, they smote them hip and thigh as relentlessly as their prototypes had smitten the Philistines. If in the course of such a history, the heathen retaliated and burned a village, a monument upon that spot would only perpetuate the memory of a gigantic wrong. In our own colony, the early record was but little different. At times, under the Dutch rule, the outlying settlements were plundered, and once, even Manhattan Island was almost made a waste. But follow the uprising of the Indians to its origin, and there was always back of it the crime of the dishonest or the outrage of the fiendish white man.

But the massacre at Cherry Valley was of no such character as this. It was not bred from injustice or outrage to the Indian. It was an outgrowth of the Revolution, pure and simple. It was but one, although the most marked, of a series of tragedies in which the people of Central New York sealed in blood their devotion to the cause of human liberty. It has been overshadowed by the massacre at Wyoming, which occurred a few months earlier, but even these two events were much dissimilar. Wyoming was settled by a colony from

Connecticut, which, without right, claimed a large tract of land located within the borders of Pennsylvania. This alone led to a petty civil war, in which the settlement was destroyed three several times before the Revolution. Again, the land in dispute between the whites had been reserved by the Indians for a hunting ground. It was claimed by them that a pretended conveyance obtained by the Connecticut company, was executed only by a few unauthorized sachems, who had been plied with liquor. The attack upon the settlement made in July, 1778, was led by the hostile white claimants to the land, and was joined in by the Indians, who for years had been complaining bitterly of the wrong done to them.

For the massacres in Central New York, of which that at Cherry Valley was typical, no such provocation or pretence of one existed. The lands here had been purchased in good faith, the Indian title had been quieted, and there never was an adverse claimant. No injustice or wrong had been perpetrated upon the red man. On the contrary, the most friendly relations existed between the races ; and among the inhabitants of this valley, Brant, the Mohawk chief, numbered some of his dearest friends.

It is this peculiar character of the event which we commemorate to-day which gives to it historic interest. It illustrates a phase of the Revolutionary struggle which was almost unknown outside of Central New York, which is little understood, but without which the history of that great conflict is very incomplete.

To comprehend the whole bearing of the story, two considerations must be kept in view—the geography of the country and the character of its inhabitants.

Look at the map of the thirteen Colonies, and you will see that New York is fitted to its place like the keystone of an arch: at the lowest angle it touches the ocean, while its northern frontier stretches along the St. Lawrence and the lakes. Nor is this all. Remember that Canada was always hostile, and see how the settlements of New England were protected by an

almost impenetrable forest, while the Colonies to the south
and west had New York between them and the foe. But
look again at the map, and you will discover something of
more importance in New York's history. On the east you
will see the waters of Lake Champlain, which flow to
Canada, almost mingling with the head-waters of the Hud-.
son, which empties into the Atlantic, while the Mohawk
cuts the triangle east and west. Now recall the fact that
the colonies had no great highways but the lakes and rivers,
and you will appreciate New York's position. Nature gave
her the key to the American continent, and almost from
her earliest infancy hostile nations were striving for its mas-
tery. Following this view of the geographical situation
a little more in detail, we shall see the paramount importance of Central New York in Colonial history and the
Revolutionary struggle. Trace up the Mohawk to its source,
and we find its waters almost confused with the streams which
run northward into the lakes. Step over the narrow range of
hills which bound the Mohawk on the south, and we come to
the great water-shed of the country, on whose slope the
streams arise which make up the Delaware, the Susquehanna
flowing into Chesapeake Bay, and the Ohio which empties into
the Mississippi, and thence into the gulf of Mexico.
To this natural configuration of Central New York is largely
due the predominance of the Five Nations whose long house
stretched along the Mohawk. When the Europeans landed in
America, they found this powerful confederacy of the native
tribes acknowledged as conquerors from the great lakes to
Georgia, and from the Atlantic to the Mississippi. Other tribes
were hemmed in by mountains, or by boundless barren wastes,
but no such barriers impeded their conquests. Launching
their light canoes on the streams which flowed from their
hunting grounds as from a mighty fountain, in time of need
they could hurl an overwhelming force upon almost any foe.
By nature the bravest and most relentless of the Indians,
a long career of conquest had intensified their native traits.
Sage in counsel, wily in diplomacy, and fearless in battle, they

have well been called the Romans of America. The English recognized their prowess, and in very early days made with them treaties of alliance ; not as conquered tribes, but as sovereign nations they acknowledged the kings of England as their superior lords. It was through their conquests that the English claimed a title to the vast territory in the West, which years later was successfully enforced against the pretensions of the French.

Remarkable as was New York's geographical position, still more peculiar was the character of her population. In this she differed from all her neighbors ; they, for the most part, were settled by a homogeneous people, but New York was always cosmopolitan.

First in time stand the Dutch—heroic men, who came in an heroic age. We never can over-estimate their influence in the history of American liberty. Their New England neighbors sometimes sneered at the Dutchmen; but Motley, a New England historian, has taught the whole world to do them honor. Defeating in the open field the trained legions of Spain, the great military power of Europe ; building up a navy which made them masters of the sea ; establishing the first great republic ; taking as their motto, Taxation only by consent ; and enforcing the doctrine of universal religious toleration, they were fit men to lay the foundations of the Empire State. Mingling with them came French Huguenots, men who chanted psalms as they went into the battle of Ivry with Henry of Navarre, who, driven from France, blighted by their absence the country which they left. These, with accessions from the more liberal thinkers of New England, made up the population of the eastern and lower portion of the province.

But it is in the people of Central New York that we to-day are chiefly interested. And here we encounter two other races that have left deep impressions on the world's history—the Germans and the Scotch-Irish.

Late in the seventeenth century, Louis XIV., seeking universal dominion, invaded Germany. The Rhenish Palatinate,

whose inhabitants were mostly Protestants, was swept over
by his armies as with a tempest of fire. Prosperous towns
and thriving cities were blotted out, and whole districts made
a desolation. The homeless people, nearly naked in the
depth of winter, were set adrift and scattered to the four
quarters of the earth. Large numbers of them took refuge
in England. Thence, in 1710, about three thousand emigrated
to New York. They had been promised aid by the government in their settlements, but these promises were mostly broken. Left to shift for themselves, many went to Pennsylvania;
but the rest, making their way into the interior, settled along
the Schoharie Creek and on the upper waters of the Mohawk.
They were an industrious, active, prudent people ; among
them were men of learning and capacity, and when the Revolutionary struggle came, they were surpassed by none in
devotion to the cause of liberty.

Thus far, every settlement made in New York, except those
upon Long Island, had crept along some navigable stream of
water. Now a new departure was to be taken, by pushing
across the range of hills which bounds the Mohawk on the south.
This was reserved for a race perhaps the most remarkable of
all the pioneer settlers of America. I refer to the Scotch-
Irish, who have given to this country John Stark, Robert
Fulton, James K. Polk, Sam Houston, Horace Greeley, John
C. Calhoun, and Andrew Jackson. "World-conquering,"
they have well been called ; certainly, when they plunged
into this wilderness, they needed all the energy and nerve
which have made the blood so famous.

In 1738, Lieutenant-Governor George Clarke made a grant
of about eight thousand acres of land in this section to four
gentlemen, one of whom was probably his own representative,
as was customary among officials in those simple days. Shortly
after, three of the grantees assigned their interest to John
Lindesay, one of their number, and the Lieutenant-Governor. In 1739, the patent was surveyed and divided, Clarke
receiving his portion, part of which his descendants own
to-day.

To the white man this whole region was then an unbroken wilderness; but to the Indians it was familiar ground. The Five Nations, which, by the accession of another tribe, had now become the Six Nations, had a colony at Oquago, on the Susquehanna, in the present county of Broome. To reach that place from the Mohawk they came through this valley, struck the Cherry Valley Creek, and thence in their canoes could float down the Susquehanna.

Mr. Lindesay, who was a Scotch gentleman of some distinction in the colony, attracted doubtless by the beauty of the scenery, concluded to take up his residence upon this spot. He selected for a farm a tract of land just below the present village, now occupied by Mr. Joseph Phelon. There with his family he passed the ensuing winter. The season proved severe, even for this climate ; the snow fell to a great depth ; their provisions gave out, and starvation stared them in the face. Haply they had cultivated the friendship of the natives, and at the critical moment, an Indian appeared upon the scene, probably passing from Oquago to the Mohawk. Learning the condition of affairs, he hastened on his snowshoes to the river settlements, and thence bore, on his back, food for the helpless pioneers. Thus here, as elsewhere, did the savage welcome the European with acts of kindness; and I am glad to say that here the kindness was repaid by gratitude and justice.

The experience of this winter almost discouraged Mr. Lindesay, but the next year he was cheered by the arrival of about thirty Scotch-Irish settlers, from Londonderry, in New Hampshire, led by the Rev. Samuel Dunlop, a Presbyterian clergyman and a graduate of Trinity College, in Dublin. From that moment the success of the little colony was assured. The men who had left their homes for religion's sake were not to be daunted by hardship; they who had passed through the siege of Londonderry were to be affrighted by no dangers. Their first step was to build a church in which to worship God; next their leader opened a classical school for the education of their children. Thus the valley was dedicated to Religion, and her hand-maid, liberal education. This was the first church west of the Hudson in which there was preaching in the English language, and the first classical school of central or western New York.

Down to the outbreak of the French and Indian war in 1755, the settlement had grown but little, yet it had more than held its own. That conflict, which proved the training school for the war of Independence, threatened it with annihilation. A part of the Six Nations, composed of the more western tribes, proved unfaithful to their English allies, and hovered over the frontier like a dreadful portent of ruin and desolation. At one time it seemed as if Cherry Valley must be abandoned till the return of peace, but the erection of some rude fortifications and the stationing of a company of rangers in the place averted the necessity. Yet, even at this period, with the torch lighted for the destruction of their homes, and the tomahawk sharpened for their wives and children, these brave pioneers turned out for distant fields of service. In the famous campaign of 1757, a nu nber of them were in the provincial army commanded by Sir William Johnson, at Fort Edward. Even after the Revolution the survivors of these veterans could hardly restrain their tears, as they told of the massacre at Fort William Henry, caused by the cowardice of the regular English commander, who forbade Johnson and his militia from marching to the relief of their beleaguered comrades.

By the termination of the war which gave to Great Britain the whole continent to the banks of the Mississippi, the infant settlement felt relieved from danger. Thenceforth its increase was more rapid, but as compared with the magic growth of towns and states to which we are accustomed in modern days, it was yet extremely slow. The whole section south of the Mohawk was almost a wilderness. The hills were rugged, the winters long and bitter, and the soil not so inviting as that along the Mohawk and the Hudson. Still, by its streams rich bottom lands were found, and like the creepers of a climbing plant hidden in the knotted bark of some great forest tree, here and there a bunch of leaves, a blossom or a bud, gave signs of growth. Down the creek which rises here within the sound of my voice, and forms the chief branch of the Susquehanna, the settlers took their way, planting a little colony at Otego, another at Sidney Plains near Unadilla, and following up a tributary stream founding the beautiful village of Laurens. Still further down and on Charlotte Creek, the eastern branch of the Susquehanna, the renowned Harpers from Cherry Valley planted the settlement of Harpersfield. Across the hills to the west Springfield was founded at the head of Otsego lake, and to the southwest Newtown Martin, which we now call Middlefield. In the other direction towards the north they made a little settlement at Bowman's Creek, half way down the hills to the Mohawk. Over on the east, but a few miles distant, the sturdy Germans had cultivated the valleys of the Schoharie, and of the Cobleskill, while the Mohawk, as far up as the present village of Herkimer, was alive with an active, industrious, thriving people. These settlements formed central and western New York, at the outbreak of the Revolution.

To-day this portion of the State contains a vast population; but we are not to imagine that it bore any such appearance a hundred years ago. Cherry Valley, which was the centre and parent of the settlements along the Susquehanna, contained only about three hundred inhabitants. The others were much smaller, some of them being composed of only a few scattered families. In 1772 the county of Tryon was carved out of the old county of Albany. It embraced all that part of the State lying west of a line drawn north and south nearly through the center of the present county of Schoharie. Its entire population was estimated at ten thousand, of whom not more than twenty-five hundred could have been capable of bearing arms. Now remember that the Six Nations alone, who lived around and among these people, numbered over two thousand brave and skillful warriors, while in the whole department there were over twenty-five thousand savages trained to the use of arms, and you will gain a faint idea of what it meant when the yeomen of Central New York espoused the cause of liberty.

2

From the close of the French and Indian war, Indian outbreaks in New York had been a thing unknown. The policy adopted by the English after the conquest of the province in 1664, was intended to secure this result, but as the colony grew in numbers and pushed itself out on every side, it is questionable whether it could have been accomplished, except for the genius of one man, and this man deserves here more than a passing notice.

Early in the last century Sir Peter Warren, an English admiral, who married the sister of James DeLancey, Chief Justice of the province, purchased a large tract of land in the Mohawk Valley, about twenty miles west of Schenectady. To superintend its settlement and sale, he sent to Ireland for one of his nephews, William Johnson, a young man of twenty-three years of age. This youth settled upon his uncle's tract. He opened a store and traded with the natives. He purchased land in his own name, and soon acquired a fortune. Broad-shouldered and atheletic, fond of wild sports, inflexibly honest, and truthful to a proverb, the Indians soon came to love him as a brother. The government recognized his ability, made him superintendent of Indian affairs, commander of the frontier militia, and a baronet of Great Britain.

His history reads like a romance. There is nothing like it in the Colonial annals. A scholar, understanding French and Latin, sending to Europe for rare engravings and the latest works on science, we find him at times dressed in Indian costume parading among the dusky warriors like a native chief. In the broad halls of his noble mansion on the Mohawk, the Six Nations were always welcome guests. They felt at home, for Sir William could converse with them in their native tongue. There they would sometimes gather in hundreds, and although surrounded by unguarded stores of what to them were treasures of untold value, their host never lost the value of a farthing. In all their controversies with individuals or the government he protected his Indian wards, as in ancient Roman days the tribunes stood between the people and the oppression of the nobles. If anything more was needed to raise him in their estimation, it was found in the connection which he formed with Molly Brant, the sister of the great Mohawk chieftain, who has written his name in blood and fire all over the valleys of Central New York.

The influence of Sir William Johnson over the Indian tribes was almost unbounded; among the Six Nations, in particular, his word was law. Added to the weight of his private character was the fact, that, as superintendent of Indian affairs, he represented to them the sovereignty of Great Britain. Annually he distributed the presents which the mother country with sagacious liberality lavished upon her savage allies. Nor was his influence confined to the native tribes. He was hardly less powerful among the whites. In 1764 he founded the village of Johnstown, erected there a baronial mansion, and gathered about him a colony of Catholic Scotch Highlanders. Other settlers flocked in, and when Tryon county was created in 1772, his town became the county seat. He married in early life a daughter of one of the Germans in the Mohawk Valley, and his relations with these people were always intimately friendly. The whole population looked up to him as a leader, consulted him on all important affairs, and never found their confidence misplaced.

Such were the character and position of Sir William Johnson. No man in America equalled him in influence; no one except the proprietor of Pennsylvania was the owner of such vast estates. Had he lived, the history of Central New York might have been very different, for it is questionable whether he would have unloosed the savage hordes about him upon the friends of his youth and manhood. But in July, 1774, just as the conflict opened, this great man died. His title and estates descended to his son Sir John Johnson, the superintendency of Indian affairs fell upon his nephew and son-in-law, Colonel Guy Johnson, both of whom were very different characters from the man whom they succeeded. The old baronet had made his own fortune, had grown up with the valley, and sympathized with the settlers about him; the young men were bred to wealth and luxury, and looked down on poverty and toil.

The old man, though made a British baronet, never forgot his youth, and is said to have keenly felt the wrongs of his adopted country; the young men were scions of the aristocracy, and felt only the wrongs of their own order. Sir William was the benefactor of his valley; his son and nephew became its scourges, and their names have been pilloried in history.

Neither of the young men who now came upon the stage possessed the ability or the influence of the man whose loss the whole colony deplored. Yet they were active and untiring, and from their wealth and position wielded a power only second to that of their predecessor. Colonel Guy Johnson had been selected by his uncle to succeed him as superintendent, and took the position with all the prestige of a mighty name and the warm gratitude of the Indian tribes. Sir John was a man of less ability, but the Tories of the valley, who were rich and powerful, looked up to him as their natural leader.

Such was the position of affairs in July, 1774. The month previous the Boston Port Bill went into operation. The friends of liberty in New York City had suggested a Continental Congress. Already the storm of approaching war was visible around the whole horizon. Men less brave than the settlers of Tryon County might well have hesitated as they looked into the future. At Johnstown, barring their communication with the eastern portion of the province, lay Sir John and Colonel Guy Johnson, with five hundred Roman Catholic Scotch Highlanders, Tories to the core ; all along their northern frontier stretched Canada, whose loyalty to England was never doubted. Water communication on the east and on the west laid them open to the incursions of the foe, while in their midst dwelt an enemy of equal numbers with their own, whose weapons of war were the torch, the tomahawk and scalping knife.

But these men never faltered. In August, 1774, they held a large meeting at Palatine to express their sympathy with the Bostonians, and their concurrence in the plan of a Continental Congress. The resolutions put forth on that occasion are worthy to stand with any adopted in the thirteen colonies. We are loyal to King George, they say, but we insist upon our rights as English subjects, which are so sacred that we cannot permit their violation. We can be taxed only with our own consent ; any other method is unjust and unconstitutional. They pledged themselves to unite with their brethren in the rest of the colony in anything tending to support their rights and liberties, and engaged faithfully to abide by the conclusions of the approaching Congress. Early in the spring of 1775, the Tories at Johnstown drew up and circulated an address avowing their opposition to the measures adopted at Philadelphia. At once meetings were called all through the county to protest against this action, and one of the largest and most enthusiastic was held in Cherry Valley. On the appointed day, the little church was filled with the patriotic people. Even the smaller children were taken by their parents that they might be baptized with the air of freedom. At this and similar gatherings, articles of association were subscribed denouncing the proceedings at Johnstown, and pledging the subscribers to the support of Congress. A few days afterwards the Palatine Committee wrote a letter to the committee of Albany, describing the peculiar condition of affairs in Tryon County, asking that no ammunition should be sent there unless consigned to them or persons whom they should name, . and concluding with the words, " It is our fixed resolution to be free or die." These were high-sounding but not empty words. With their lives, the men who wrote them redeemed their promises.

Meantime the Johnsons were fortifying their homes along the Mohawk. Still no act of violence was committed by their partisans, and the friends of liberty thought it advisable not to precipitate a conflict. The Indians had not risen, and Colonel Guy Johnson, the new Superintendent, declared his purpose to maintain their neutrality if possible. Indignantly he disclaimed the idea that he could be capable of setting the savages on his peaceful neighbors; and yet while the words were upon his lying lips, he had received secret instructions from the crown to induce the Six Nations to take up the hatchet against the king's rebellious subjects. Few things in history equal the infamy of these instructions, which we now know emanated directly from King George the Third. In the French wars the case had been very different, for the French themselves always employed their Indian allies. But the employment of the savages by the English in the Revolution, while the Americans only sought to keep them neutral, has no excuse or palliation.

At first Colonel Johnson made little headway in following out his orders. He called an Indian counsel at his residence, but felt himself so hampered by the suspicious men about them, that he removed to Ontario with his whole family and retinue. With him there went two persons of great influence among the Indians the one was Molly Brant, with her eight children by Sir William Johnson; the other was her brother, the famous Joseph Brant, Thayendanegea.

Brant was a full blooded Mohawk chief, tall, erect and princely in his movements. Educated at an English school in Connecticut, he had lived much mong the whites, but never lost his native traits. Education, instead of enfeebling, only made him a more fearful foe. He possessed the self control of the white man, with the endurance and the cunning of the savage. The tales of his cold-blooded cruelty are doubtless fictions, for he showed at times a true nobility of character. But in the heat of battle he was terrible. For years to come his name along the border almost made the boldest shudder. He seemed to bear a charmed life, his movements no one could divine, but his blows were as unerring and as swift as fate. In 1776 he was made principal war chief of the confederacy, but now he was secretary to Colonel Guy Johnson, and in that position rendered efficient services. At Ontario another council was held and his Majesty's work was soon accomplished. All the Six Nations, except a few Tuscaroras and about half of the Oneida tribe, pledged themselves to support the English cause. Thence, Col. Johnson passed into Canada, secured the services of seventeen hundred of the northern confederacy, and then took up his residence in Montreal. Sir John Johnson still remained at home, but in the next year it was determined to disarm the Tories in the Mohawk Valley, and he was arrested and liberated on parole. Shortly after he shamelessly broke his parole, and also fled to Canada. Thereafter he only meditated vengeance on his countrymen.

Still for sometime Tryon county suffered little. Many of the Six Nations had gone to Canada with Col. Johnson; the more bitter royalists, among whom were the wealthy Butlers, had done the same, and although rumors of Indian invasions were heard on every side, none actually occurred. But this was felt to be only the calm before a storm. The Declaration of Independence had been hailed with great joy throughout the country, and peace it was known could now only be attained by force of arms. The inhabitants organized into companies, erected rude fortifications about their houses, and prepared for the approaching contest.

In 1777 the storm broke upon Central New York.

Thus far the colonial war for independence had been almost an unbroken series of disasters. Now the English government concluded to make one grand effort and end the struggle. New York was recognized as the key to the continent; could it be captured, the other States might be mastered in detail. To effect this object, a campaign was planned in England with great elaboration. It was resolved to send out three expeditions, one under the commander in chief, to start from New York and follow up the Hudson; another under Burgoyne, to march from the north by the way of Lake Champlain; and the third under St. Leger, to start from Oswego, and go down the Mohawk Valley. The three armies when their work was done, were to meet at Albany, and the confederacy would be cut in twain. The scheme was well conceived, and but for the valor of Tryon County it might have been successful. Sir John Johnson had represented to the British government, that the Tories in the Mohawk Valley were in the majority of five to one, and that it needed only the presence of some regular troops to cause a general uprising. These were furnished, and they were the picked of the English army. With them marched Sir John Johnson, and his regiment of Tories, burning for revenge, Colonel Butler of the Mohawk and his Tory rangers, and the Six Nations led by Brant. Patiently they had bided their time, and now at length it had arrived. Had they been successful, had they swept down the valley with the prestige of victory, swelling their forces as they marched, and bringing to Burgoyne the supplies of which he was in such bitter need, no one can say that Saratoga would have witnessed the surrender of the British army.

When the news went down through the Mohawk Va'ley that St. Leger with his force of British troops, Tories and Indian allies were on the march, offering a reward of twenty dollars for every American scalp, the whole people were aroused. On the way from Oswego and upon the site of the present City of Rome, stood Fort Schuyler, the old Fort Stanwix, of the French and Indian war, held by seven hundred and fifty continental troops, commanded by Colonel Gansevoort, of Albany. St. Leger saw that he must take this fort or nothing would be gained. The delay was unexpected, for it was supposed that the place was out of repair and would fall without a blow. When the army encamped before it, the summons went out to the patriots of Tryon County to hasten to its aid. At once eight hundred men flew to arms. They were mostly Germans, for the notice was so sudden that only those living in the upper Mohawk region had time to reach the field. But three men from the Cherry Valley settlements joined the expedition — Colonel Samuel Campbell, Major Samuel Clyde, and Lieutenant Robert Campbell. The two former were members of the Committee of Safety of Tryon County, and probably were in attendance at a meeting in the valley; the last, who lost his life in the subsequent engagement, lived at Bowman's Creek.

Of the battle of Oriskany, which turned back the tide

threatening the Mohawk Valley with destruction, I have little time to speak. A year ago, seventy-five thousand people on the battle ground listened to the story from abler lips than mine. They heard how the eight hundred yeomen led by Herkimer fell into an ambuscade. How they fought for life, and yet wrested victory from the jaws of death. How, when the sun went down, St. Leger's expedition had received its death blow. How the Mohawk Valley was saved and Burgoyne's last hope was swept away. Washington said "Herkimer first reversed the gloomy scene" of the campaign. General Schuyler and General Gates praised the victors for their courage, and General George Clinton, just inaugurated the first Governor of New York, thanked them, in behalf of the new-born State.

This is the story of the triumph, but I have another tale to tell. The battle saved the Mohawk Valley to the patriot cause, and I concur in all that was said a year ago regarding its importance, but it brought upon Tryon County for the next four years a storm of fire and blood, by which it was nearly blotted from existence. The causes of this we have not far to seek. Although the Indian tribes had two years before pledged themselves to support the British cause, they had thus far been rather lukewarm. They had many friends among the patriots, and could not see any advantage to themselves in a war between the whites. Brant, to be sure, felt otherwise, for he was a captain under English pay, but he could not carry the confederacy beyond a general treaty of alliance. When they joined the army of St. Leger, it was solely upon the promise of Sir John Johnson, that there should be no fighting, simply scalping and plunder without danger to themselves. But the battle of Oriskany changed all this. In that engagement and the sortie from Fort Schuyler, the Indians lost nearly a hundred of their bravest warriors. This loss they swore should be avenged, and fearfully they kept their oath. Again, the Tories who had fled to Canada, had waited patiently for two years, expecting the time to come when, with a British force, they could return, and

3

taking possession of the valley re-occupy their homes. The opportunity had come, but had only proved that their hopes were false. To them, too, nothing but revenge was left. They swore to ruin where they could not rule. Among them were brave and able men; aided by Brant, whose efforts were unceasing, they now found no difficulty in inciting the savages to slaughter. Alone either party would have been comparatively harmless, united they ranged like fiends over the whole of Tryon County. The cold-blooded atrocities perpetrated on their prisoners by the Tories and Indians after the battle of Oriskany gave a foretaste of the future. Spurred on by the whites, the savages put their unresisting captives to death with all the tortures that ingenuity could devise. Not satisfied with this, it is said that they roasted the bodies and ate the flesh.

In the autumn after the battle, occurred a few scattered outrages, but in 1778 the bloody drama opened which made Tryon County a wide waste of desolation.

And now we come to the events which took place here. To both Indians and Tories, Cherry Valley was an object of bitter hatred. Here resided John Moore, who was the delegate to the Provincial Congress from Tryon County, and particularly obnoxious for his earnest stand for Colonial Independence. Here also lived Colonel Samuel Campbell and Major Samuel Clyde, both members of the County Committee of Safety, and surpassed by none in patriotism, energy, and zeal. They were skilful Indian fighters, and had done great execution in the battle of Oriskany. After the fall of Herkimer, Colonel Campbell had been left the highest officer upon the field, and at the close of the engagement was in command of the American forces. The other residents of the town were not inferior to these men in love of liberty. Probably no place in the United States has such a Revolutionary record as this frontier town. It numbered as I have already stated only about three hundred inhabitants, and yet in 1776, with the neighboring settlement of Middlefield, which contained but a few scattered families, it furnished thirty-three soldiers to the patriot army ; one out of every ten of its inhabitants, men, women and children.

As the central and largest settlement south of the Mohawk river, the people of the surrounding country had early flocked to it for safety. A rude fortification had been thrown up around the walls of Colonel Campbell's residence, which occupied the place where his grandson's house now stands, on a side hill commanding a full view of the valley. Into this primitive fortress the people had gathered in time of danger, and the presence of a company of rangers had thus far secured their safety. But in the spring after the battle of Oriskany, General LaFayette, who was in the Mohawk Valley, appreciating the importance of the position, directed a fort to be constructed in the town.

This fort was subsequently erected, but meantime an incident occurred which lights up with a touch of humor a picture which is otherwise monotonously sad. Early in May, Brant had planned a descent upon the settlement, having been informed that it was at that time without a guard of soldiers. Stealthily approaching through the forest with his hostile band, he gained without detection the summit of a hill which bounds the valley on the east. Looking down from this height, to his utter consternation, he beheld a company of troops parading on the green in front of Colonel Campbell's house. Satisfied that he had been deceived, he concluded to abandon his attack; when, at a later day, he learned the truth, even his stoic calm must have been somewhat moved. The doughty warriors whose appearance had so astonished him, proved to be a company of little boys, the children of the settlement, dressed out in paper hats and armed with wooden swords and guns.

But the day which began in comedy had a tragic ending. Unable to reconcile the evidence of his own senses with the information which was brought to him, Brant passed a little to the north, and took his station near the beautiful Falls of the Tekaharawa, some two miles distant from the village. That morning, Lieutenant Wormwood, a son of a wealthy patriot of Palatine, and personally a friend of Brant, had come up from the Mohawk River, bringing the intelligence that Colonel Klock would arrive the next day with a part of his regiment of militia. Late in the afternoon he started to return, accompanied by Peter Sitz, the bearer of some dispatches. Throwing down his portmauteau, he mounted his horse, saying, " I shall not need that, as I shall return to-morrow with my company." His to-morrow never came. A few minutes after their departure, his horse returned alone, the saddle stained with blood. From behind a rock which stands near the romantic falls, Brant had appeared and commanded them to halt. Disregarding the order, they had put spurs to their horses, and tried to pass. A shot wounded Wormwood, and as he fell Brant rushed forward, and, mistaking his old friend for a Continental officer, tomahawked him with his own hand. Sitz was captured, but managed to destroy the, dispatches showing the true state of the garrison. He gave up a false set which he carried; and Brant being now assured of his mistake, went on, and Cherry Valley was left in peace.

During the summer the fort was constructed, which had been ordered by General La Fayette. It was a rude structure, built by the inhabitants themselves, but sufficient for frontier warfare. Located just below the present village, it encircled the church and the plot of ground used then and now as a graveyard. Within its walls the people stored their valuables, and themselves took refuge. Going out to till their fields, one party worked, while another stood guard with loaded muskets. About them the air was heavy with dreadful news. In June, Brant and his savages had burned the neighboring settlement of Springfield. In July Colonel John Butler, with some fiendish Tories, and a band of Indians, had desolated the beautiful Valley of Wyoming. About the same time, a force of four hundred and fifty Indians, invaded the Valley of the Cobleskill, and laid it waste. A little later McDonald, one of the Johnstown royalists, with three hundred Indians and Tories, had ravaged the Schoharie Valley, and early in September the extensive and populous settlement of the German Flatts had been burned by Brant. Yet Cherry Valley remained untouched, and as the autumn passed on the inhabitants breathed more freely, for they knew that in winter the Indians were rarely found upon the war-path. Some who had left the settlement returned and those who remained began to relax their vigilance. The movements of Brant justified their conduct. In October, feeling that his summer campaign was ended, he made his way towards Niagara, to go into winter quarters. Unfortunately, before he reached his post, he met the man to whom the Cherry Valley massacre is due.

Just after the battle of Oriskany, Walter N. Butler, son of the Tory colonel, John Butler, was arrested at the German Flatts, for endeavoring to incite a rising among the people in favor of the crown. Tried by court martial as a spy, his offense was clearly proved and he was sentenced to be shot. Unfortunately his life was spared through the intercession of some of his early friends, and he was kept a prisoner at Albany. Thence he escaped in the summer of 1778, and joined his father at Niagara. Panting for revenge, and emulous of the fame which his father had won by the massacre at Wyoming, he eagerly sought an opportunity to show that the son was not unworthy of such a sire. With these objects, although the season was far advanced, he planned an expedition against the settlement at Cherry Valley, obtained the command of two hundred of his father's Tory rangers, and permission to employ the Indians under Brant. The Mohawk chieftain, whom he met returning from the east, was at first reluctant to serve under such a leader, but was finally persuaded to join the Tories with five hundred of his warriors. The little army thus swollen to seven hundred men, made its way through the lower portion of the State, and striking the Susquehanna, ascended its waters towards the doomed settlement.

The approaching force was overwhelming, and yet the final tragedy might have been avoided, save for the ignorance and folly of one man. The fort, which mounted four guns, was garrisoned by an eastern regiment numbering between two and three hundred soldiers. It was large enough to contain all the inhabitants, and would have afforded them a secure place of refuge. On the eighth of November, a messenger from Fort Schuyler brought intelligence of the hostile expedition. At once the people begged leave to move into the fort for safety. But the commanding officer, Colonel Ichabod Alden, of Massachusetts, denied their prayer. The refusal was not due to inhumanity, for he himself lodged without the fort. He was simply ignorant of Indian warfare, presumptious, and like many greater men despised the savage foe whom he had never met. Promising the inhabitants that he would take measures to advise them of the approach of danger, he put out scouts in all directions. The party sent down the Susquehanna, partaking of the disposition of their Colonel, on the evening of the ninth, kindled a fire, and all lay down in peaceful sleep. Towards day-break they awoke to find themselves surrounded and disarmed. On the night of the tenth, the enemy encamped on a thickly wooded hill about a mile southwest of the village. On the morning of the eleventh they moved from their encampment toward the fort.

Colonel Alden and Lieutenant-Colonel Stacia, with a small guard, lodged at the house of Mr. Wells, which stood on a little eminence just below the village. The place had formerly belonged to Mr. L'ndesay, and is now owned and occupied by Mr. Phelon. Some of the other officers also lodged in private houses The enemy, learning these facts from the scouts whom they had captured, disposed their force so that a party should surround the residence of each officer, while the main body attacked the fort.

Even the elements combined against the hapless settlement. The night before, snow had fallen to the depth of several inches ; in the morning it turned to sleet, and the air was dark and heavy. The people, trusting to the assurances of Colonel Alden, were resting quietly at home, unconscious of approaching danger. One man only was abroad. He lived several miles below the fort, and was coming to town on horseback. When a short distance from the house of Mr. Wells, he was fired upon and wounded by the Indians. Putting his horse to full speed, he turned out of his way to inform the Colonel of their approach, and then hastened to alarm the fort. Still Alden was incredulous ; he thought it was but a party of stragglers, and sent out orders to call in the guard. Before his order could be obeyed, the Indians were upon him. The advance was formed mainly of the Senecas, the most untamed and blood-thirsty of the Six Nations. Now, at length, the Colonel realized the danger, and fled down the hill toward the fort. Behind him followed a fleet-footed savage, with uplifted tomahawk. Several times Alden turned and snapped a pistol at his swift pursuer, but in the damp air the treacherous weapon failed him. At last the fort was nearly gained, its doors stood open for his reception, when the Indian's tomahawk, hurled with unerring aim, cleft his skull. As he fell, the savage rushed upon him, knife in hand, and, under the very muskets of the soldiers, tore off his bleeding scalp.

Meantime, at the house of Mr. Wells, a dreadful scene had been enacted. When the savages rushed in, the father of the family was engaged in his devotions, but a Tory slew him while he knelt at prayer. With him perished his wife and mother, three children, his brother and sister, and three domestics. One daughter, endeared to all by every christian grace, escaped from the house and sought safety behind a pile of wood. She was pursued by an Indian, who, as he approached, wiped and sheathed his bloody knife and drew his tomahawk. Having some knowledge of the Indian language, she begged piteously for life, and a Tory who had formerly been a servant of her father interceded for her, claiming to be her brother. With one hand the savage pushed aside the Tory, and with the other smote her to the earth. Of this whole family, but one escaped the carnage. He was a young boy who was absent in Schenectady at school. Thus his life was spared. He grew to manhood, and settling in New York, made the name of John Wells famous as the foremost lawyer of his time. Looking down upon the desolation of his homestead, he might have said with Logan, " there runs not a drop of my blood in the veins of any living creature." Like Logan, however, he was fitted alone to represent a race.

Another party of Indians surrounded the house of Mr. Dunlop, the venerable clergyman whose ministrations the colony had follow d from its cradle. Through the intercession of a Mohawk chief, the old man's life was spared, but only that he might witness the fiendish murder and mutilation of his wife, and the destruction of his little flock. Carried away prisoner, he was soon released, but within a year went down to his grave broken with age and sorrow.

One other incident and I nave done with these sickening details. I tell them that you may know what border warfare meant in Tryon County ; that you may know what our fathers meant when they said they were " resolved to be free or die." A Mr. Mitchell was absent from his house when the Indians came. Finding return impossible, he fled to the woods for safety. When the fiends had departed he approached his home, and there a fearful sight awaited him. He saw before him the bodies of his wife and four children. Extinguishing a fire which had been kindled to destroy the house, he bent over his little ones, hoping that life might still remain. In one, a girl of ten or twelve years of age, a spark seen d yet to flicker ; he raised her up, brought her to the door, and with beating heart was watching over her return to life when another party of the enemy appeared. He had hardly time to hide himself behind a log fence near by, when they approached the house. From his hiding place he beheld an infamous Tory named Newbury, bury his hatchet into the skull of the little girl. The next day the desolate father all alone bore the five corpses to the churchyard, and with the soldier's aid buried them in a common grave. I am glad to say, that the following year Newbury was arrested in the Mohawk Valley as a spy, convicted on the testimony of Mr. Mitchell, and hung as a common malefactor.

The victims of the massacre numbered about forty-eight in all, sixteen of whom were Continental soldiers, the rest were mostly women and children. The fort was not taken, for the assailants had no cannon, and Indians rarely attempt to carry fortifications. During the day, several attacks upon it were made, but successfully repulsed. Outside of the fort, however, the whole country was laid waste. Houses and barns, with all their stores were burned, the cattle were driven off, and nothing but smouldering ashes marked the site of the once happy settlement. From the mere list of those who lost their lives, no idea can be gathered of the misery inflicted. Some families escaped and wandered almost naked to the Mohawk. Others, and these were the larger number, were taken prisoners, and felt themselves reserved for a fate much worse than death.

As I have already said, three of the citizens of Cherry Valley were particularly obnoxious to the Tories ; they were John Moore, Colonel Samuel Campbell, and Major afterwards Colonel Samuel Clyde. These three men all escaped, the first two being absent from home, the last being stationed in the fort. Their families, however, were considered as only second in importance to themselves, and special arrangements were made for their capture. Fortunately the wife and children of Colonel Clyde escaped, and fleeing to the woods, remained hidden all day and night under a friendly log. The families of Mr. Moore and Colonel Campbell were less fortunate. The former were taken without resistance. In the case of the latter a fight was made that excited even the admiration of the savages. Mrs. Campbell's husband was absent, but her father, Captain Cannon, who lived at Middlefield, was visiting his daughter. He too was a member of the Committee of Safety, was an old sea captain from the north of Ireland, and never dreamed of surrendering without a blow. As he was all alone, except some negro slaves, he knew that a defense of the house would be useless, and would only endanger the lives of those entrusted to his care. But resolving to sell his life as dearly as possible, he sallied forth, with a stock of muskets, and a negro boy to load, and took position behind a tree which stood below the house. As the savages approached he poured into them a rapid fire, until a bullet in the leg brought him to the ground. When the Indians rushed up they found that the force which

4

had opposed their progress consisted of one old man. Happily he was recognized, and his position, with admiration for his gallantry, saved his life. The house was then surrounded, and Mrs. Campbell with her mother and four children were taken prisoners. Her eldest son was saved through the devotions of his negro nurse, who wrapped him with the family Bible in a blanket and hid them behind a fence. When the father returned to his home this was all that was left of his family treasures.

As evening fell the enemy gathered up their plunder and prepared for a departure. The prisoners, drenched by the rain and with no protection against the wintry blast but the scantiest apparel, were huddled in groups and marched down the valley. About two miles below the fort they halted for the night. Around them gleamed the watch-fires of the savages; far in the distance rose the smoke from their burning homes, while within their hearts dwelt sad forebodings of the future. At length dawn broke to their sleepless eyes, and again they resumed the march. The aged mother of Mrs. Campbell, unable to keep pace with her companions, was tomahawked by her Indian guard and thrown naked by the road side. Her daughter, bearing an infant in her arms, was driven along by the same demon with uplifted and bloody hatchet.

The next morning a halt was called and the joyful news communicated that it had been determined to send back the women and children. However, the families of Mr. Moore and Colonel Campbell were excluded from the act of grace, and reserved for a long and rigorous captivity among the Indians. The mothers were separated from their children, and it was not until near the close of the war that they were exchanged and reunited with their families. Six years ago we laid to rest the last survivor of this party. A lad of four years, when he was taken prisoner, he remembered almost to his death the incidents of his Indian life. During the late civil war one of his grandsons was taken by the Confederates and confined at Andersonville. As the old man heard how these prisoners were treated by their Christian captors, he used to say, that on the whole, he thought the red man was the least savage of the two.

On the morning after the massacre, a party of Indians returned to glean the bloody field, but two hundred militia arrived from the Mohawk, and they soon dispersed. Then followed the sad work of burying the dead. From the scattered ruins of their homes the charred and mangled corpses were gathered up. In the old church yard a deep trench was dug, and there in a common grave most of them were laid down to eternal rest. Upon this spot we have to-day erected our monument. It stands not to record a triumph, but that future generations, as they read the inscription upon its stone, may remember what it cost to win the liberties which sometimes we prize so lightly.

When the inhabitants, who had escaped, met again at the fort, and were joined by the prisoners who had been released, it was determined to abandon the settlement. Their homes were in ashes, all their property, except the bare land, had been destroyed, and to attempt rebuilding would only invite another raid, against which, from their exposed position, they had proved so powerless. Under the circumstances most of them moved to the Mohawk Valley, and there during the continuance of the war they did noble service. In the summer the fort was given up as useless, a band of marauders applied the torch to the old church, and Cherry Valley existed only as a recollection.

In the year after the massacre at Cherry Valley, General Sullivan conducted an expedition against the villages of the Six Nations. One part of his force passing from the Mohawk to Otsego Lake dammed its waters, and floated down the Susquehanna on the flood caused by opening the dam. Turning to the west they dealt a blow to the Onandagas, the Cayugas and the Senecas, which it was hoped might give Tryon County peace. Yet even in this very summer Cobbleskill was again ravaged, and frequent murders along the frontier showed how insecure was life.

But in 1780, the bloody work reopened on a gigantic scale

and continued down to the return of peace. First the little settlement of Harpersfield, the last of those along the Susqu.- hanna, was blotted out, and then the valleys of the Schoharie and the Mohawk west of Schenectady, were made a desolation. I have neither time nor heart to dwell upon these scenes, in fact it would be but a repetition of the story which I have already told. In the various settlements rude forts had been erected, twenty-four in all, into which the inhabitants flocked for safety. But in the whole district outside their walls was hardly left a building or a breathing living thing.

Yet you must not imagine that the sturdy patriots of Tryon County witnessed the destruction of their homes with- out resistance. After the battle of Oriskany, they saw full well what the future had in store for them. Writing to Con- gress they pointed out the dangers of their exposed position ; showing how without a regular force it would be impossible to protect the frontier against the Indians, but closed by saying, " We are resolved if we do fall to fall as becomes brave men." Nobly did they redeem their pledge. Time and time again they gathered and drove the invaders from their soil. The records are stained with fire and blool, but never with dis- honor.

The town of Sharon but six miles distant, witnessed one of the bloodiest minor engagements of the war. A party of one hundred and fifty militia, led by Colonel Willet, whom the Indians called "The devil," with the brave Major M'Kean of Cherry Valley as second in command, utterly routed a hostile force of twice their number. A few months later occurred the battle of Johnstown, equally creditable to Tryon County. There Willet, with about five hundred men, defeated a force of Tories outnumbering his own, exclusive of some one hun- dred and thirty Indians. In the rout which followed this victory, Walter Butler, the author of the Cherry Valley mas- sacre, lost his life. With poetic justice he met the very fate which he had meted out to others. Fleeing up the Mohawk he reached the West Canada Creek, across which he swam his horse, and then turned to bid defiance to his pursuers. An

Oneida Indian who, like a sleuth houn1. had followe1 on his
track, with a rifle ball brought him wounded to the ground.
Casting aside gun and blanket, the Indian plunged into the
stream and swam across. Butler now piteously begged for
mercy. The Oneida, brandishing his tomahawk, replied in
broken English, " Sherry Valley, remember Sherry Valley!"
and then cleft his skull.

These were about the only occasions on which the patriots
could drive the enemy to an open fight. But the record is
illuminated throughout with individual deeds of daring such
as history cannot surpass. The world's tales of romantic valor
contain nothing more absorbing than the lives of Murphy,
M'Kean, Harper, Shankland, Shell, the Sammonses and Captain Gardenier. The story of their adventures would make
the fortune of a novelist.

But against the enemy with whom they had to deal, valor,
discipline and skill were powerless. Around them and in their
very midst lived secret spies who gave notice of their every
movement. To the Indians each foot of the surrounding
country was familiar ground. They marched without baggage
and by secret paths, and never knew fatigue. Behind them
stretched illimitable forests, into which they would retreat
when they had struck their blow. They never wanted for
ammunition for Canada and the British forts were unfailing
arsenals. Besides this they now were fighting for their homes
and hunting grounds, and the Tories, the bloodier of the two,
had no future except revenge. Under such conditions it is no
wonder that Tryon County was made a waste. What her
patriot people suffered, the world can never know. Bare
figures give but a faint suggestion, and yet they tell a fearful
tale. Of the whole population it was estimated that about a
third went over to the enemy, of those remaining one-half
were driven from the country or died by violence. At the
outbreak of the war, the county contained twenty-five hundred able-bodied men, at its close it numbered twelve hundred
taxable inhabitants, three hundred widows and two thousand
orphans.

Such were the sufferings of the loyal men of Tryon county; but looking at the grand result, they were not borne in vain. Their homes were ruined, their property destroyed, and at times gaunt famine threatened them with utter extermination; but they held the Mohawk Valley for the Continental cause. Beyond them lay Albany and the district of the Hudson, from which our army largely gathered its supplies. Had the Mohawk been surrendered, the Hudson would have been the frontier of the State ; and what that meant, Tryon County knew. But those twenty-four little forts, scattered along the Schoharie and the Mohawk, were never taken. About them blazed the fires and gleamed the tomahawks of the savage foe ; around them bloody raids were made ; but no army marching to the Hudson could leave such fortresses behind it. This gave to the county its strategical importance. But another consideration should not be overlooked. When, after the surrender at Yorktown, England made peace with her rebellious colonies, it was not so much on account of any defeats which she had suffered in the field, as because it was apparent that a people like this could never be subdued. Among this people, whose indomitable spirit thus wrung from England a reluctant peace, you will find none whose record for valor, constancy and fortitude surpasses that of the patriots of Tryon county.

I feel that I have given but a very imperfect sketch of what Central New York did and suffered in the Revolution. Yet read your school books, and of this you will scarcely find a trace. Read your more pretentious histories, and you will be told that New York had a large Tory population, and you will find little else besides. This is very true, but it is the merest fraction of the truth. It is only the dark setting of the picture, which should throw into the sunlight the glorious colors upon the canvas. No where were the Tories so active and untiring : but nowhere did, the patriots do and suffer so much as here.

I am ashamed that New Yorkers have let other men write American history and make the picture of the shadow. With her capital, the whole of Long Island and Staten Island and most of Westchester county, in the hands of the enemy; with the central portion of the State such as I have pictured it, the wonder is that New York ever did anything toward the Revolutionary cause ; and yet of the thirteen States three only furnished their full quota of men to the Continental Army, of these New York was one ; but two furnished their full quota of money and supplies, of these New York was one. She was the only one of the thirteen that furnished her full quota of men, money and supplies.

Prior to the Revolution she was always foremost. She first resisted the oppressions of the crown ; she first made stand against the power of Parliament ; she led in resistance to the Stamp Act ; her merchants signed the first non-importation agreement ; her citizens organized the first committee of. correspondence; she first suggested Colonial Independence; upon her soil the first blood was shed in the Revolutionary struggle, and within her border was fought the turning battle of the war. And yet historians have called her lukewarm. She first founded the freedom of the press ; she first established full religious toleration ; by her magnanimity she formed the first confederation of the States ; she gave to the Supreme Court its first Chief Justice ; she gave to America its first and greatest financier ; and yet her history has been substantially ignored.

But I believe that all this is coming to an end. With the records now accessible, every student knows the truth. Such gatherings as we have witnessed in the State during the last two years, show that the people are interested in the subject, and where there is knowledge and a desire for information coexisting, the two must come together. One thing I think New York in justice to herself should do. She now has a population much larger than that of the whole thirteen colonies at the time of the Revolution. She has a history of unsurpassed importance. It should be made a study in every school-house in the State. The political system of this country is peculiar. In certain departments the General Government is supreme ; it has exclusive control of commerce ; it alone can make war or peace, coin money, and the like ; and as supreme in these relations, every one studies the history of the United States, and is acquainted with the Federal Constitution. But in the larger circle of internal affairs, upon which the daily welfare of the citizen depends, the State is equally supreme. It is somewhat like the family circle, in which husband and wife are one, and yet each is a responsible independent being. A good American citizen should understand the history and Constitution of the United States ; but as the citizen of a State, he should understand its history and Constitution. When this is done New York will take her right position, not alone in history, but in the councils of the nation.

And now a few words more, and I have done. When the Revolution had closed, the scattered and broken inhabitants of Cherry Valley returned to their deserted homes. Exiles they called themselves, and well they might. They brought back from their wanderings nothing but stout hearts and the air of freedom which they breathed. But, nothing daunted, they began life over, and soon prosperity smiled upon the little valley. They were a God-fearing people, those early patriots. When in 1775 they received a summons to a Sunday meeting of the Committee of Safety, they replied that as the business was not urgent in its character, they could not forego attendance on the public worship of their God. Now that they had returned from exile, they met in the old graveyard, and there upon the soil which contained their sacred dead they reorganized their church. The first pastor was the great man of whom I have already spoken, the famous Dr. Nott, of Union College. As the settlement was in its infancy devoted to the cause of liberal education, so it continued in its riper years. Here was located the celebrated Academy, in its day the best known institution of its kind in the center of the State. Until the canal and railroads had diverted travel and population, its lawyers were the leaders of the bar, and its physicians have always been pre-eminent.

The last half century has worked great changes in its for-

tunes; but I am proud to say that its people have not proved
unworthy of their ancestors. A century has not thinned the
strong red blood that coursed through the veins of the early
patriots. We have to-day erected a monument in memory
of those who a century ago died to give us liberty. Our other
monument in the public square commemorates the sacrifice of
those who died that it might not perish from the land. During the Revolution, the little town sent out more than one-tenth of its population to the Continental Army. I believe
that no other place in the United States has such a record.
How many went forth in the late war, no one seems to know;
but the facts within our knowledge tell a tale which it is hard
to equal. At the breaking out of the Rebellion, the town
numbered about two thousand people ; it furnished to the
Union army six lieutenants, eleven captains, and ten officers
of higher grade ; nearly if not quite enough for a regiment of
a thousand men. In the old graveyard lie the bodies of thirteen soldiers who died in service, while the bones of thirty-two
others are known to lie on Southern battle fields. Doubtless
this does not complete the tale, for some died in prison, and
others sleep in unknown graves ; but if forty-five were all, it
would yet make a glorious record. One death in five enlistments is a large percentage. Measured by this standard, the
little town must still have furnished to the army more than a
tenth of its total population.

To such a people I need hardly speak of the lesson taught by
the event which we to-day commemorate ; it has already come
to them from the free hills by which they are surrounded, and
the sacred soil beneath their feet. These, with the air they
breathe, have been more eloquent than tongue of man.
Her sons have shown how dearly they prized their fathers'
Union by the joy with which they went to battle for it.

But a century ago the sacrifice was not ended when the
war had closed. Our fathers returned to find ashes where they
had left their homes ; weeds and underbrush in place of cultivated farms. Others might have been discouraged ; they,
with valiant hearts, began their life anew. Not only did they

suffer in the war itself, but while they lived the sacrifice continued. After a century, history repeats itself. Our brave soldiers saved the Union, but their sacrifice is not yet ended. At home the fathers and mothers nobly did their part, but their work is not yet done.

The Revolution left these valleys a waste of desolation : our war has left us an enormous debt ; has prostrated our trade, and crippled industry. Our work will not be done until true prosperity is re-established, and our debt is honorably paid. Men who during the Rebellion were secret traitors to their country talk of repudiation, though they gloze the term with specious words. Communists from France, and Internationalists from Germany, preach the destruction of society. To some men these are attractive sounds. The signs about us seem to presage a conflict as momentous as any by which we have been tested. But as New York has always in the past proved a bulwark in time of war, I trust that she may now stand as a bulwark against national dishonor. People who have no history can perhaps afford to repudiate their debts, as men who have no character can afford to be dishonest ; but New York can be placed in no such category. Certainly we here could not thus prove unworthy of our ancestry. Our fathers, our sons and brothers would rise from their graves as witnesses against us, if we refused to bear our part of the sacrifices in the cause of liberty. We complain of our taxation and the bitter pressure of the times ; but think how this valley looked at the close of the Revolution. Let us be, like our ancestors, patient, brave and honest ; let us trust in the God who has guided our nation from its cradle, and we shall see the return of a durable prosperity based on honesty, justice, and respect for law.

www.ingramcontent.com/pod-product-compliance
Lightning Source LLC
Chambersburg PA
CBHW021449090426
42739CB00009B/1691